THE

HAGGADAH

OF *LOVE*

A Ritual to Celebrate Love

By Marilyn Bronstein & Philip Belove

In Memory of Philip

This book is dedicated to Philip Belove, my co-creator and close friend, who passed away December 30, 2014 while we were working on this project.

Acknowledgements

Many thanks to everyone who helped us put the Haggadah together.

I particularly want to thank my three magicians: Cedric Speyer, Mona Wizenberg and Helga Schleeh who, with their editing, designing, and tech skills, helped turn my dross into gold.

Thank you to all who contributed their inspirational works of art: Miriam Lanail, Therese Weinberger, Leona Heillig, Violaine Dasseville, Tzippy Corber, Sarah Bronstein, Graziella Malagoni, David Scribner, Mona Wizenberg, Nicole Miritis, and Helga Schleeh,.

Thank you to Emmanuel Delaportas for his Art Photography that appears on the front and back covers.

Thank you to Philip Belove who set me on this journey and then somehow left me to carry on the work down here, while he is up there, working on our next book, *Angels in Love*.

And finally, thank you to my love-partner, David, who has been my greatest teacher in love.

Links:

Emmanuel Delaportas	http://www.studioemm.com/
Helga Schleeh	http://www.helgaschleeh.com/
Sarah Bronstein	http://www.recycollagedesigns.com/

Celebrating Romantic Love

Today we are gathered to honor romances.

"CUP OF JOY"

Artist Miriam Lanail

Romances are stories. That is what the word 'romance' means; it means stories about what happens, the accomplishments, the challenges and the set-backs along the way.

But today is not about just any kind of story. We are speaking today of romances of love, how love changes peoples' lives, not only the life of the couple, but also the lives of those around them. Such stories are sacred and perhaps that is why they are often guarded and rarely shared in community. Today some of these stories will be shared, so we will be on sacred ground and we must remember that.

These stories are alive. That is why they must be told and retold every year. With each telling, if we stay within the sacred space, the stories evolve into more and more complex forms. As we hear them we also evolve.

This ritual is for all of us. Today we are gathered to witness Love's possibilities. There are people here today who have experienced love deeply, people who are just beginning to experience it and people who have not yet found their b'sherte (their soul mate).

If you have been lucky enough to find love, if love has taken you where you've never gone before, it's important to share your experiences. People need to know what's possible.

This ritual is based on the Passover Haggadah, a tradition which might be more than 3000 years old. This tradition says that we need a story-telling ritual every year to remind us of the gift of freedom. How much more so do we need a ritual every year to remind us of the gift of Love?

So let us gather every year to retell our love stories.

Note to the leaders of the seder :

The Haggadah provides a basic structure for the ritual but it's important that each group makes this ritual personal. Please feel free to modify as it suits you.

As we go through the four questions, each question is designed to elicit a personal story. In this Haggadah we have provided stories drawn from the authors' research, especially their books, *Rabbis in Love* and *Old Enough to Love Better.* We hope that people will also share their own stories. This is a gift, and also a risk. This is time to share stories, not advice. Not everyone has to share, but please remember, when we speak of the love that two people share, we are on sacred ground. Privacy and boundaries must be respected.

Ideally the group should be a mix of single people looking for love, couples freshly in love and couples who have been together for a long time and may need their love refreshed and enlivened.

Participants should bring food for the ritual. We will want four platters prepared, each one to be used in a different part of the ritual:

Platter One: To remind us of the anticipation of love. Bring foods with exquisite aromas. These would include fresh herbs and soft spices, flowers and fresh greens, fragrant oils, too.

Platter Two: To remind us of the transforming power of love. Bring foods that have been transformed: aged cheeses, breads, olives, pickles; anything that's been changed from its original state.

Platter Three: To remind us of the challenges of love... bring something with strong flavor: Spicy, pungent, bitter or sour: Ginger, Kim chi, wasabi, horse radish, chilies. Use your imagination.

Platter Four: To remind us of the constantly refreshing pleasures of love... bring fruits to dip in chocolate or caramel. Also, natural aphrodisiacs like dates, mangos, lychees and pomegranates.

In addition, to remind us of the intoxicating power of love, bring wine. (or juice if you don't want to drink wine.)

The ideal number for this gathering is between 8 and 14 people. It also works well as a private evening for two or a large group.

Participants may be invited to contribute their own love poetry and songs. They should also be encouraged to ask questions about love,

Depending on the size of the group, plan on a four to five hour evening to allow everyone to participate.

The Threshold
Lighting the candles and the invocation

We are now crossing a threshold.

There are miracles in this life we take for granted, or even deny, and one of the loveliest is the love between two people. We need to remind ourselves of what's possible and anticipate it with great gratitude.

Today, we will share stories about love and longing. Because we are speaking of matters of the heart, there will be many times when each of us is touched in private ways. Let us allow for those moments. Let us offer time and silence to savor them.

So let us begin. Let us talk about love. Let us speak from our hearts.

For most of us, this is a realm apart from everyday life, so let us mark the boundary between where we are going and where we ordinarily live.

(Leader lights the candle)

Welcome to the Haggadah of Love.

Artist Marilyn Bronstein

Learning to Love

"PASS THE HONEYCAKE"
Artist Miriam Lanail

Yearning to love with a heart that's pure
Discerning what's love when a mind's unsure
Burning to love where there'll be no cure
I'm learning, learning to love.

Uncover my mind and my heart lies there
Uncover my heart and my soul lies bare
Uncover my soul and there's nothing there
And we'll stare in the fires of love.

Somewhere we go over the rainbow
Past where the pot of gold lies.
Beyond stories, blue morning glories
Reflecting me in your eyes.

Take me to love with a hand that's sure
Awake me to love with a heart that's pure
Make me to love where there'll be no cure
Teacher, guide me, come here beside me,
We're yearning, we're burning, we're turning, returning,
We're learning, learning to love.

(Music & lyrics by M. Bronstein)

6

When it comes to learning about love, the sages talk about four different kinds of people.

Artist Marilyn Bronstein

The first type worries about getting it right. They want advice. They ask, "What am I doing wrong?" or better still, "What is my partner doing wrong?" To them we say that tonight we're not going to list "the top ten things you must do to have a perfect relationship." Instead we are going to hear stories, true stories from people in this room. And we will see how stories can answer questions we didn't even know to ask.

The second type echoes the sentiments of 'Rabbi' Tina Turner when she sings , "What's love but a sweet old-fashioned notion … who needs a heart when a heart can be broken?" To them we say, "If that voice prevailed, you wouldn't be here, today. The stories you hear, today, will strengthen another voice in your head, or your heart, one that still believes that love is possible. And that it is possible for you."

The third type is in love with love, but a greeting card picture of love. For them, if the road isn't smooth, it's not love. To them we say, "True romance involves the whole story, the good times and the bad. We're going to share stories about all of this, the challenges as much as the gifts.

The fourth type doesn't like any of this talky-talk about love. They are deep believers but they think talking about love trivializes it. "It's too private, too intimate to share with outsiders." To them we say, "'Love allows us the privilege of being close,' to quote Rabbi Cahana. There are so few opportunities to share intimate stories about love. Some of you here today are blessed to have a great love in your life. What an act of generosity it is when you grant others the privilege of being up close to that love."

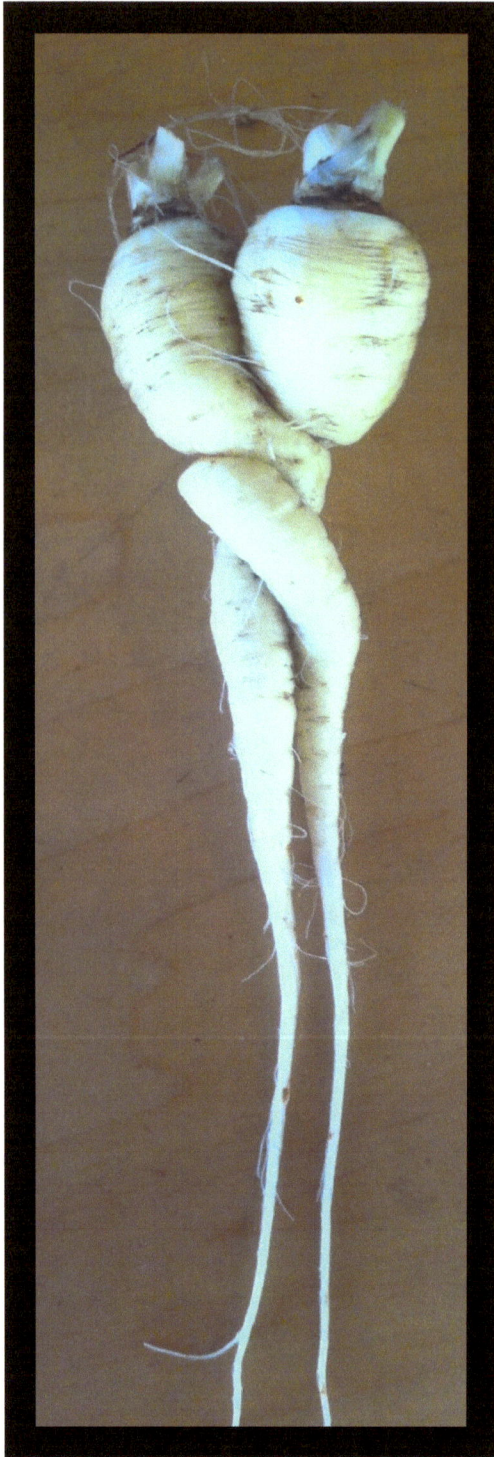

Whether you are single, whether you are newly mated, whether you've been partnered for years, we all need reminders of love's possibilities.

Grown & Photographed by David Scribner

Acknowledging the Hidden

(for this ritual, everyone will need paper and colored pencils)

Close your eyes. When it comes to love, most of us have a yearning so deep we can barely name it. As we begin, we are going to pay attention to that deep desire. It's there now, an image, a sense of how we want to be in love and how we want love to be. We're on an inward search for something personal, intimate, and specific. Let the vision emerge. Be patient. There will be hints, a fleeting image, a sensation, a feeling.

Try to capture it on paper: a phrase, a symbol, a word, a color, a hint of what that private yearning is for you. Now, everyone have something? Now fold the piece of paper and hold it up and say these words in a quiet voice.

Artist Marilyn Bronstein

"This is The Hidden, a small piece of something so close to my heart that I hold on to. This is my 'Afikomen,' the piece that is hidden until the end of the ceremony." Now we hide it on our person. For each of us, may this gathering make us more aware of secret yearnings and holy longings.

9

How do we begin to talk about love?

Artist Leona Heillig

The world is filled with sacred things that we take for granted. Today we are going to stop and notice them and appreciate them.

Romantic love starts with the realization that this particular story, the one unfolding right here, right now, with this particular person, is sacred. In its textures and promises and challenges it is unlike any other relationship. It touches what is most unique and individual within our own story.

And so we ask ourselves ...

(Chanting) *"Why is this relationship different than all other relationships?"*

This question is at the heart of our ritual. Asking it is like opening the ark and finding ourselves face-to-face with something sacred. But how do we talk about it? How do we answer that question?

By asking four more questions.

Who here will ask the four questions about love? The most innocent? The most doubting? The one who thinks about it the most? Or the least? The one who can chant the best? If you feel summoned, speak up!

(It can be a single person, a couple, or a group)

The Mah Nishtanah (The Four Questions)

(Chanting in traditional melody)

How is this relationship different from all other relationships?

When did you first realize that this relationship had sacred possibilities?

How did this relationship take you to places you never thought you would go?

How does this relationship challenge you and make you grow even further?

How do you reconnect with those sacred possibilities when you're caught up in the humdrum of daily life?

The Telling of Romance

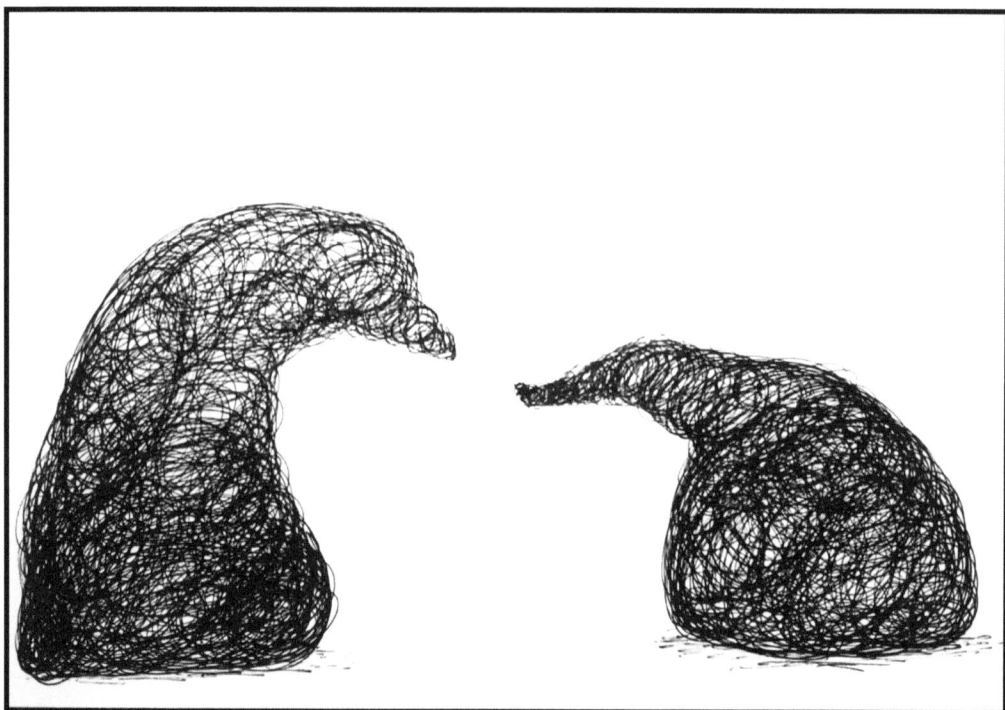

Artist Leona Heillig

These questions are to be answered with stories. It's time for the Telling. Some of you will be speaking your stories; others will be listening; a story needs both. When a story is shared, it transforms both the teller and the listener.

Now is the time we open our hearts and share memories of moments that touched us and changed our vision of Love's possibilities and challenges. Let us be both generous and receptive.

The First Cup: The Annunciation

Artist Therese Weinberger

(everyone fill their cup)

This first cup is for those moments when we are first touched by love's arrow.

There are memories we cherish of those first moments.
Let us lift our cups: To the first graces of love.

(bless & drink)

And now let us share stories.

(Ask for 2 people to read the story or ask someone in the group to share their own story of when they first realized this person was going to be significant in their life)

What do Rabbi Shefa Gold and Rachmiel O'Reagan have to say about their 'first hint of love'?

Shefa: I knew right away.

Rachmiel: I was a little slower. We had met briefly in October. She had just moved here and asked me to show her around the Valley. And I said, "I'd love to. When do you want to get together?" And she flipped through a little calendar in her book. This is October. I'm a local guy and, I'm thinking next week. She said, "How does December 20th work for you?" And I said, "What?"

Shefa: I had a very busy schedule.

Rachmiel: So that gave me a clue right away. But in the meantime, right after my birthday, November 18th, we happened to be in the same local restaurant together.

Shefa: Actually Rachmiel was with another woman, I was with another man and we saw each other across the crowded room. And we...

Rachmiel: I went, "Oh, that's the woman I just met. Oh, Shefa."

Shefa: So we just kind of floated towards one another and there was this big – I don't know – a very powerful hug that happened.

Rachmiel: It was the first hug. We had never even hugged before.

Shefa: And we didn't even know how that happened. And...

Rachmiel: We had our partners back at our tables.

Shefa: And I came back to my table and the guy I was with said, "Who was that who just mauled you?"

Rachmiel: And my friend and I – we weren't in a relationship, just really good friends – she said, "Wow, who is she? Who is that?" And I said, "Wow, I don't know, that was so – I was just going to go say hello to her and we were just hugging."

Shefa: Just pulled into a vortex. It was just a startling kind of moment. We didn't know what that was about.

Rachmiel: Totally mutual, like, "Wow!" and totally unexpected. So I knew it was very special the first time we hugged . We were in the Star Trek beam. I can still feel it.

Shefa: And then, after our first date in December, I went to this hot spring resort and got a massage. Immediately this great presence, who identified himself as Eliahu, came into the room. And said to me, "Up until this moment you've been on the path of fission, a kind of a breaking of the heart, where the yearning moves you towards God. But," he said, "There's a new door opening and it's a door to the path of fusion. You have a choice now whether you want to walk through this door." So immediately at that moment Rachmiel's face appeared in my mind and I knew that he had been sent to me to be my partner on the path of fusion. I think that was my moment of knowing.

Rachmiel: So then, when were together on New Year's Eve at the end of December of '99...

Shefa: I said, "Let's do a kissing meditation." So we set up my meditation room like the Tree of Life with candles at each of the points. There was a big window and we sat in front of it and we looked out at the valley. At the stroke of midnight, as we entered into the New Millennium, there was a bursting of our relationship. And whatever love was between us was going to be sent out to the world. And then the next day, I called up all my friends and said, "This is it. I met him. This is it."

(excerpt from Rabbis in Love)

The Anticipation Ritual

Sometimes we get a whiff of the future, that's especially so with relationships.

Now, it's time for sharing: Time for foods that wake up the palate.

(pass around the first platter)

Artist Mona Wizenberg

Let us each take a leaf of fresh herbs or a flower. Let the smells waft over us. Let us acknowledge that wonderful, primitive part of our being that senses what is coming before we name it.

And as we do that, let's ask ourselves the first question: For either a current or past relationship, when did the sacred possibilities of that relationship first dawn on you? When did you first realize that this was going to be a significant person in your life?

Close your eyes, and recall a time you hold in your mind like a picture or an oil painting. What was happening between the two of you at that moment? What were you wearing? What were you thinking or feeling? If you imagine it as a movie scene, how did it play out?

While we share appetizers, who wants to share their first 'knowing' moment? We want just one moment in time so pick the best one.

(Allow time for a few people to share their stories in small groups or with everyone)

Had we unlimited time, we could spend hours teasing out the threads of these stories and how these snapshot moments contain some of the fundamental themes of a romance about to unfold. But it's time for the next question.

The Second Cup: Transformation

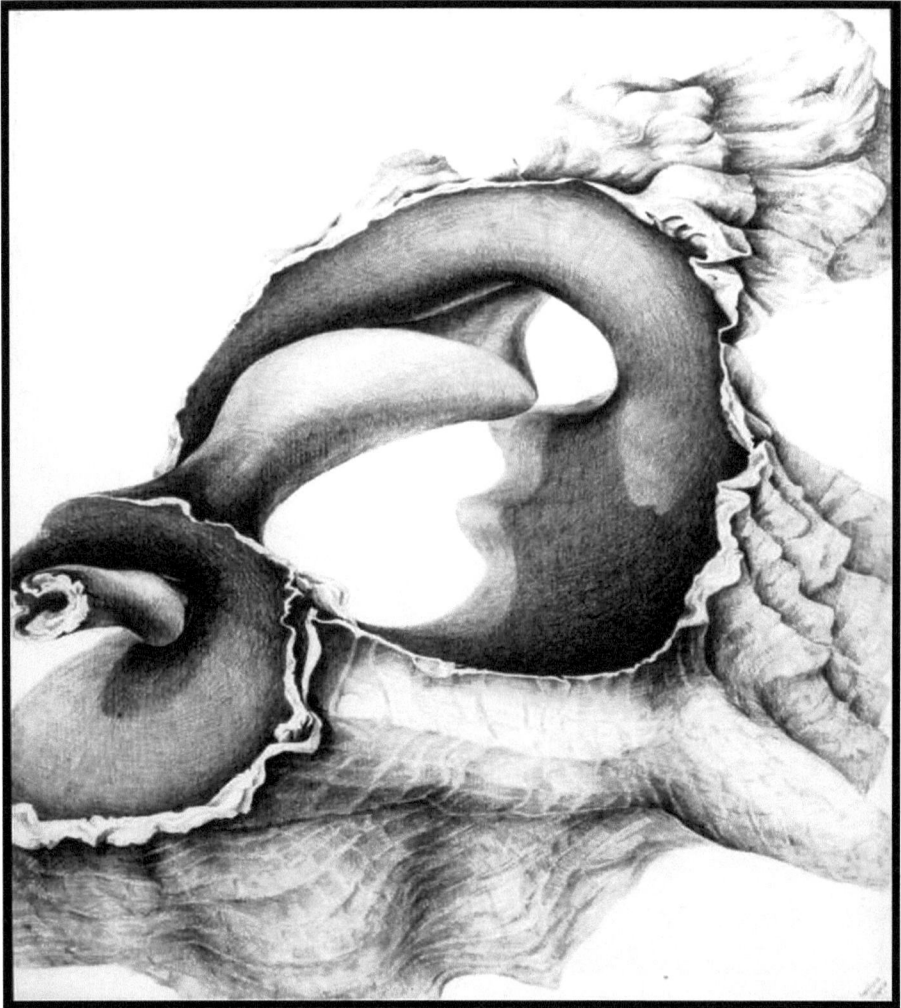

Artist Graziella Malagoni

(pour the second cup)

This cup is for recognizing how love transforms us.
Let us drink to the miracle of how Love takes us to places we could not,
or would not, go alone.

(everyone blesses and drinks)

So here we are at the second question:
How has Love transformed you?

(Invite people to share their own stories, you can skip what the Rabbis have to say otherwise choose two people to read.)

What story do Reb Haim and Rebbetzin Caroline Sherrf have about the transformative power of Love?

A little background helps. He's a Sephardic Orthodox Rabbi, used to huge family gatherings and lots of chaos. She grew up as a secular Jew on the upper West side of Manhattan, with maids and catered dinner parties. She enters his world, sort of a reverse Cinderella-story. They have eight children together.

Caroline: I didn't know what I wanted. Because of both my life experience and his coming from the culture that he did, he expected to be boss. Not that he was a despot or anything mean, but I would just naturally fall in with whatever his desires were or his wishes.

He's almost ten years older than I am. When we were younger, that was a big age difference. I had to grow up. I didn't make any demands, really, like, "Help me with the kids." I just did everything and he was busy helping everyone else.

But I wouldn't want to be married to someone who wasn't like that.

I didn't realize that I have to ask. I just assumed that he should know. I mean he's so intuitive and he's helping everyone else and I'm thinking, "Wait, hello, I'm your wife! I have needs. I need you to come, I'm tired, take the baby." But I guess he thought that I was so strong. When I had my sixth child we were having 40 guests at the time, 40 every Shabbat, plus I was going to school part-time so I said "That's it, I want full time help."

He says, "Okay, that's a good idea."

"What?" *(Chuckle)*

So I needed to grow up. So I started to make these kinds of demands—no, "requests," and then, because I started to ask, then he started to be more intuitive. Then he would realize without my asking "She needs this; she needs that." I sometimes tell girls who are newly married and who have certain frustrations "You're not making enough demands. By having your needs fulfilled, you're causing your husband to grow. It just obviously builds love."

I remember a few years ago he wrote me such a beautiful love letter: "I was a wild one but you tamed me and you taught me."

Haim: For me, one of the big adjustments was the language. In Israel, there are no smooth corners. Language is direct, short and the facial expressions suggest almost hostility. So I would be talking to my wife that way and she thinks that I'm angry with her or I'm being so bossy and I wasn't. That was just the way I grew up. So it took her time to realize that it was just a style. And it took me time to soften.

Caroline: He really softened, enormously. It's been like water on a stone. He thinks he's stubborn but I'm like an immovable object.

Haim: So somewhere we met in the middle.

Caroline: He went all the way to my side, I would say.

(excerpt from Rabbis in Love)

The Transformation Ritual

It's amazing how you can take something and turn it into something else, something even more delicious: Bread, Cheese, Wine, Partners.

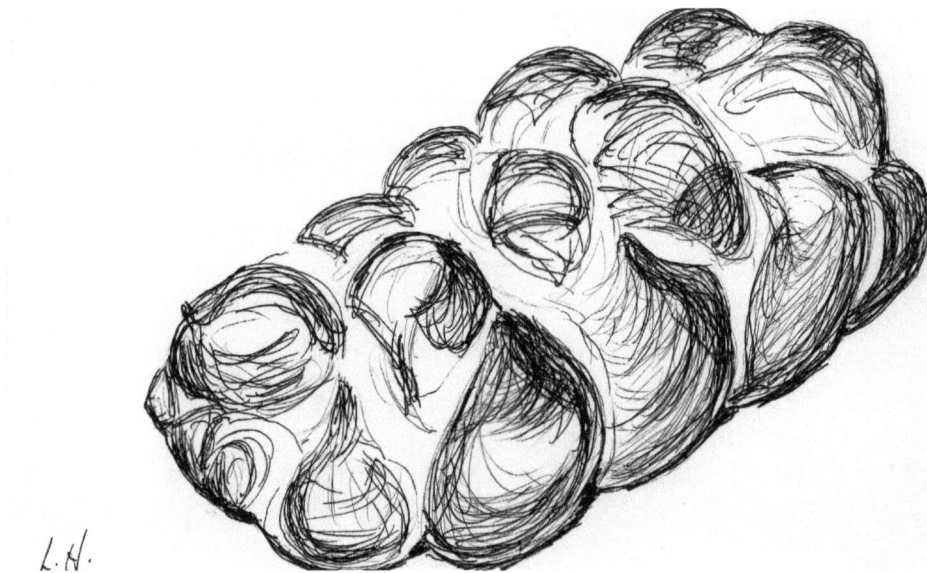

Artist Leona Heillig

(bring out the second platter and pass it around)

Let's take a little food from the platter and as we do, let's ask ourselves the same question: how has love changed you?

Picture a moment when you understood that your relationship, (current or past) had transformed you in ways you never expected.

While we share food, who wants to share their stories?

(invite people to share their stories)

The Third Cup: The Love Crucible

Artist Violaine Dasseville

Now, as we approach this part of our celebration of love, it's good that we already have some wine in us.

We're going to be asking folks to share some difficult things.

While it's true that not every challenge produces a transformation, almost every transformation is forged from a challenge. Let's pour the third cup and make a blessing: To the challenges of love and the opportunities they offer.

(everyone blesses and drinks)

And now, the third question: How has loving another well profoundly challenged you?

(Time check. If you are running out of time, skip what the Rabbis have to say and ask the group for stories to share, otherwise choose two readers)

A little background here: Rabbi Victor-and-Nadya, hyphenated, as you might note, are a couple who have been ordained as One Rabbi. They have been together 42 years.

What does Reb Victor see as the current challenge?

Victor: Well, for me, the current challenge is our age difference – nine years. That meant one thing back when we met, she was 16 and I was 25. Now, I'll be 67 in February so it's there again but in reverse. It's a whole new stage in my life.

Nadya: Victor is really in a place where he wants to consolidate and focus and retire from something. I, on the other hand, am still in producing mode and creating new programs. We've always worked together as a team.

Do I just go ahead and do these things and we don't do them as a team? Or do I focus only on projects we can do as a team and let those other projects go?

I want to support Victor in his desire and his need to slow down, but my preferred way to support him is to do a little bit more, to pick up the slack. But that's not what he wants. He would like me to slow down with him.

And so there is tension there for both of us, but we do talk about it.

And what does Reb Nadya see as the current challenge?

Nadya: The challenge for me is that Victor is a very passionate human being. He's passionate about everything even about scoring debating points. On the other hand, I keep that side of me under wraps, partly because there's this stuff inside of me that's really precious. And he really needs me to be more passionate, more expressive of that passion and I'm working on it. The question is how then can we witness and support each other at each other's growing edge.

Victor: I'm just – I'm passionately in love with Nadya. I mean, it's 42 years we've known each other. The passion hasn't...it is still fire, right? And I express it in all sorts of ways, verbally, physically, I mean, you know. And so I want it returned in the same measure even though I know ... it's not that it's a realistic expectation, it's just well, gee, what would happen if the fire, you know, if the flames were this high, if hers were this high, then it would be up that high?

Sometimes Nadya plays the legitimate role of ... not tamping down ... but tempering the passion, because it's over the top and I'm not aware of it. There are other times when it is up-tempo with her from what I am used to, and then it is a delight.

Nadya: You're also passionate about ideas, right? The passion is not just about the love, right? Whatever he's committed to, whether it is ideas or practices or anti-practices, he's very passionate, very fiery, and my stuff runs deeper and doesn't always erupt in that way, right?

So today we had an encounter that was painful because we see things going on in the Middle East very differently. And whenever these conversations come up, it's really hard because I really admire and respect and understand where Victor is coming from and I just want him to open to another perspective. I'll let him say what he really feels but I feel that he gets upset with me because my perspective maybe sounds naïve, or unrealistic. I usually don't choose to engage about these things. I'm usually silent. And when I do speak up it's hard for him and for me.

Victor: And when these things come up, for me, it's like I'm sitting on a forum and I don't know the person. It's an intellectual engagement. And for that moment, there is a kind of ... soiling of my love for Nadya. And more and more now I rein myself in. I give myself a message, "Don't go off so much because it's not worth it." And I'm getting better at that, not "just scoring debating points." You know, I was trained that way. I studied all of those years of Talmud, you know. And so, getting out of that has always been a challenge.

Nadya: We are different people. A lot of what we teach is appreciating how what seems to be the opposite in your partner is what grounds you and completes you. We've learned how to dance where we really mirror one another, where we bring opposite attributes or experiences into the relationship. And we've learned to do that dance so beautifully.

Victor: I used to think that the goal was to experience the perfect relationship, and then we came to the realization, both of us that it's not about a perfect relationship even if it was achievable. The excitement, the engagement, is in the perfecting.

(excerpt from Rabbis in Love)

The Challenge Ritual

"It's not about the perfect relationship. The excitement, the engagement, is in the perfecting." Such a good reminder. Let us each take some food here that is a bit of a challenge to eat, but also exciting. Things get a little spicier here.

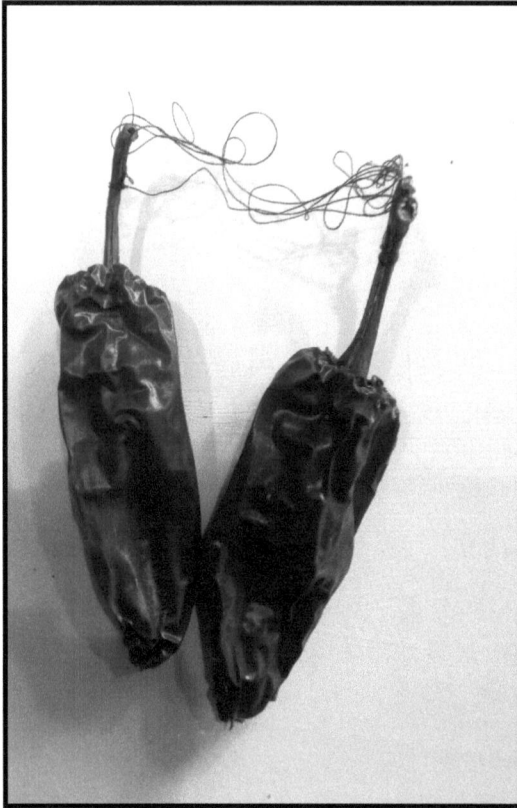

(Bring out the third platter)

Artist Tzippy Corber

As the food is being passed around, let's think about how a relationship, current or past, has tested you. Where has this relationship pushed you in a way that's really interesting?

These stories will be the easiest to think of yet maybe the most difficult ones to share.

While we share food, who wants to share their stories?

(Allow time for a few people to share their stories)

The Fourth Cup: Turn and Return

Artist Nicole Miritis

Daily life has a way of distracting us from our connections with the ones we love. How do we reconnect?

Let us pour the fourth cup and drink to the miracle of reconnecting.

(everyone blesses and drinks)

So here we are at the fourth question:

How does your spiritual practice reconnect you to love?

or

What do you do to bring you back to Love?

What do Rabbi Ronnie Cahana and Rebbetzin Karen, who have been together 36 years, have to say about returning to love?

(choose two readers)

Ronnie: I think everyone wants so deeply to be known. To be known just as is.

I think that's what's built into Shabbat, into the system of Shabbat. This is a time of eternal paradise, and it's just strolling together because 'that's the only person I want to be with'. You don't know anything. It's always courtship. It's in another realm. You have always this notion that you're just starting – I don't know anything until now. That's the greatest gift of being alive; it's being in love. And so, you start again and say, "Wow. Who are you? You're so fascinating." There's so much. I can't wait for that. Every Shabbat we bless each other. Every Shabbat we tell each other our secrets -- and their secrets.

Love allows you to live in a dimension where there's nothing but the privilege of being close. It's God's gift. And prayer prepares you. Everyday's prayer prepares you. "Oh, this is the reason for the day. This is the wondrous gift, a way I could be a part of you." So it's kind of being on the lookout for the awareness of the magic and the world opens up to us.

If we talk intimacy, which is failing all around the world, I don't want it to be our failure with each other.

Karen: So, it's to fall in love, over and over again with what I fell in love with originally. Because I think we don't change really. What we are is what our essence is. It's the 360 degrees of what I might encounter that made me look at it through one lens or another lens. But there is a space lens that sees it all. I fell in love with Ronnie through that lens, so it's to return to that place.

(excerpt from Rabbis in Love)

The Arousal Ritual

Artist Sarah Bronstein

"To fall in love over and over again with what we fell in love with originally."

How do we do that? This is the time for delectable aphrodisiacal foods... lychees, strawberries, dipped in warm chocolate.

(bring out the fourth platter)

As the food is being passed around, let's think about what you do to reconnect with the best aspects of your relationship.

Let us share some stories. What rituals have you created? What brings you and your partner back to the miracle of your love?

(allow time for a few people to share their stories)

Reclaiming the Hidden

Remember that piece of paper that we hid at the beginning of the evening? Let's each take it out of hiding. Hold on to it. Don't look at it. You don't need to. Take some herbs or a flower from the first platter and wrap the paper around it. Then close your eyes and smell it and remember it.

May the scent of your longing linger
And may it please you
And may what you've always desired
come into your life.

Artist Marilyn Bronstein

Learning to Love

Somewhere we go over the rainbow
Past where the pot of gold lies.
Beyond stories, blue morning glories
Reflecting me in your eyes.

Take me to love with a hand that's sure
Awake me to love with a heart that's pure
Make me to love where there'll be no cure
Teacher, guide me, come here beside me,
We're yearning, we're burning,
We're turning, returning,
We're learning, learning to love.

(Music & lyrics by M. Bronstein)

Artist Helga Schleeh

The Fifth Cup: The Prophet

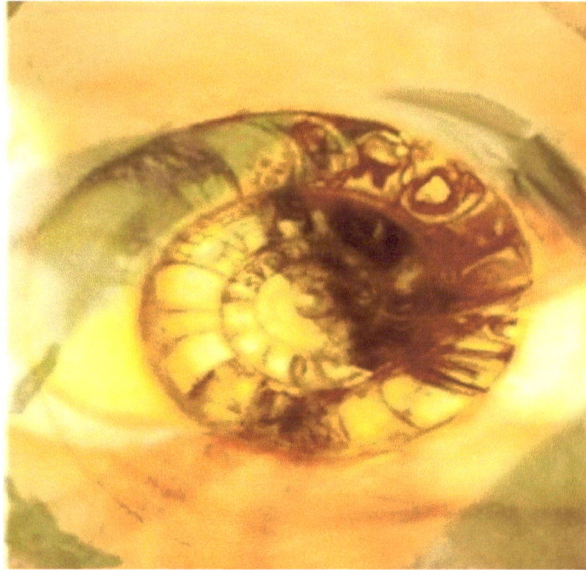

Artist Helga Schleeh

We've had our fill from the four cups yet just when we think it's over, it's time for the fifth cup. This cup is for the Prophet of Love and how we invite that Prophet into our lives. And when the Prophet is at our threshold, we must be willing to invite him/her in.

(Someone goes to the door and opens it. Meanwhile the leader places a wine glass inside a bowl and then fills the glass so it overflows into the bowl and leads the group to say the following)

Whenever and wherever people are gathered in the name of Love, Love will be there overflowing.

Now let's each take a piece of bread and soak up some of that love.
Raise the wine-soaked bread and say:

Next Year, In Love...

(play the Beatle's song, "Love is all you need," and sing along)

Love,   Love, Love
Love,   Love, Love
Love,   Love, Love

Artist Marilyn Bronstein

There's nothing you can do that can't be done
Nothing you can sing that can't be sung
Nothing you can say but you can learn how to play the game
It's easy

Nothing you can make that can't be made
No one you can save that can't be saved
Nothing you can do but you can learn how to be you in time
It's easy

All you need is love
All you need is love
All you need is love, love
Love is all you need

Love, love, love love, love,
love love, love, love

All you need is love
All you need is love
All you need is love, love
Love is all you need

Nothing you can know that isn't known
Nothing you can see that isn't shown
Nowhere you can be that isn't where you're meant to be
It's easy

All you need is love
All you need is love
All you need is love, love
Love is all you need

About the Authors

Marilyn Bronstein graduated from Maimonides College in Winnipeg where she studied with Rabbi Zalman Schachter-Shalomi and many other great Rabbis, and so began her life-long fascination with Jewish studies. She has been involved in Jewish Renewal for the last 30 years. She has animated groups, and explored the relevance of Judaism to our everyday lives through the arts. Since retiring from teaching at Champlain College, she devotes her time to the creative arts: dance, singing, music, writing, and painting. She also composes Jewish chants, and creates ritual.

Philip Belove, Ed.D., was a public speaker, workshop leader and psychologist with a specialty in relationships. "Belove" was his real name although people often suspected the name was a marketing ploy for his professional web site www.drbelove.com. His focus was always on how relationships work and play. As part of that mandate he taught tango and swing dancing. He also taught *Communication between Men and Women* at Keene State College for several years. He was a consulting psychologist with GBLA, a management consulting firm, and also maintained a private practice via internet and telephone, as well as being a relationship expert on allexperts.com .

Philip, together with Marilyn, wrote *Rabbis in Love*. They were working on their next book, *Old Enough To Love Better*, as well as this Haggadah, when he passed away on December 30, 2014.

By the Authors

Rabbis In Love is about love and what it can look like when it's a Jewish spiritual practice. This is a book about couples who are very much in love, with one of the partners being a Rabbi. *Rabbis In Love* is mainly a book of conversations and stories. It is one thing to listen to someone's advice about love and something very different to hear their stories. In this book Rabbis and their spouses speak candidly about what it's like to be married. They tell stories of how they met and fell in love and how they make their marriages work.

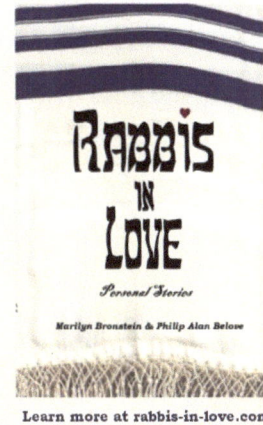

"A soulful glimpse of realistic and spiritually romantic ways for couples to relate"
Rabbi Zalman Schacter-Shalomi

RABBIS IN LOVE
Personal Stories
Marilyn Bronstein & Philip Alan Belove

Learn more at rabbis-in-love.com

"Gives you a soulful glimpse of realistic and spiritually romantic ways for couples to relate. It is a warmhearted and inspiring read." – **Rabbi Zalman Schachter-Shalomi,** author of *Davening* (Jewish Lights)

"As Rumi says, 'Lovers don't finally meet somewhere. They're in each other all along.' The love stories in this book have been with us all along, yet the authors have now done the mitzvah of allowing us to join the couples they interviewed on the journey of the heart to which we all belong." **Cedric Speyer**, M.A., M.Ed., Clinical Supervisor of E-Counseling; Creative Director of *InnerView Guidance International.*

"I love this book! In strikingly non-interventional interviews, the authors have drawn from their participating rabbinic couples emotionally uninhibited and yet delicately modest dialogues that offer us all profoundly magical, cross-culturally relevant, true stories about the beauty possible between two people, committed to each other in every way over time. It is a warm invitation, calling out to us, 'Come on in here and hear about love!'" – **Ani Meharry,** Ph.D. in Psychology, author of *Fourth Dimensional Relating: A New Frontier for the Couple.*

Books can be purchased at createspace.com, amazon.com, rabbis-in-love.com or from the author: bronste9@yahoo.com

.

www.ingramcontent.com/pod-product-compliance
Lightning Source LLC
Chambersburg PA
CBHW041554040426
42447CB00002B/177